Contents

Some words are printed in bold, **like this**. You can find out what they mean by looking in the glossary.

What are deserts like?

Deserts are large areas of dry land. Deserts can be hot or cold. Even hot deserts can get very cold at night.

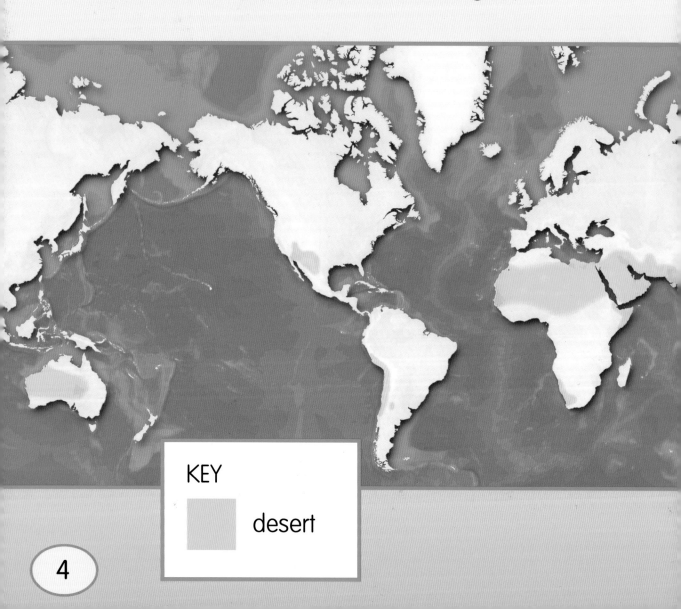

KEY

desert

HIDING IN
DESERTS

Deborah Underwood

www.raintreepublishers.co.uk
Visit our website to find out more information about Raintree books.

To order:
☎ Phone 0845 6044371
🖹 Fax +44 (0) 1865 312263
🖥 Email myorders@raintreepublishers.co.uk

Customers from outside the UK please telephone +44 1865 312262

Raintree is an imprint of Capstone Global Library Limited, a company incorporated in England and Wales having its registered office at 7 Pilgrim Street, London, EC4V 6LB – Registered company number: 6695582

Text © Capstone Global Library Limited 2011
First published in hardback in 2011
First published in paperback in 2012
The moral rights of the proprietor have been asserted.

Edited by Rebecca Rissman and Nancy Dickmann
Designed by Joanna Hinton Malivoire
Picture research by Tracy Cummins
Originated by Capstone Global Library
Printed and bound in China by Leo Paper Products Ltd

ISBN 978 0 431 01092 2 (hardback)
15 14 13 12 11
10 9 8 7 6 5 4 3 2 1

ISBN 978 1 406 22000 1 (paperback)
16 15 14 13 12
10 9 8 7 6 5 4 3 2 1

British Library Cataloguing in Publication Data
Underwood, Deborah.
 Hiding in deserts. -- (Creature camouflage)
 1. Desert animals--Juvenile literature. 2. Camouflage (Biology)--Juvenile literature.
 I. Title II. Series
 591.4'72'09154-dc22

Acknowledgements
We would like to thank the following for permission to reproduce photographs: Alamy pp. 13, 14 (© Tom Bean), 21, 22 (© Rick & Nora Bowers); FLPA pp. 6 (Bob Gibbons), 10 (Gerard Lacz); Minden Pictures pp. 17, 18 (Tom Vezo); National Geographic Stock pp. 11, 12 (Mattias Klum), 15, 16 (Bruce Dale), 25, 26 (Minden Pictures/Fred Bavendam), 29 (Michael Patricia Fogden/Minden Pictures); Naturepl.com pp. 9 (© Philippe Clement), 19, 20 (© Solvin Zankl); Photo Researchers, Inc. pp. 23, 24 (Karl H. Switak); Photolibrary pp. 8 (M Schaef), 27, 28 (John Cancalosi); Shutterstock pp. 4 (© Map Resources), 5 (© Anton Foltin), 7 (© Pichugin Dmitry).

Cover photograph of a Peringueys sidewinding adder (Bitis peringueyi) emerging from a sand dune, Namib Desert, Namibia, reproduced with permission of Visuals Unlimited, Inc. (Solvin Zankl).

We would like to thank Michael Bright for his invaluable help in the preparation of this book.

A cactus survives in the desert by storing water in its **stem**.

Deserts have very little rain. Not many plants will grow in deserts. But some plants have ways to **survive** in dry deserts.

Living in a desert

Some animals can **survive** in deserts, too. Their bodies have special **features** to help them live in deserts. These features are called **adaptations**.

The peccary can get most of the water it needs from the plants it eats.

A camel has many adaptations for life in the desert.

The camel's wide feet and very long eyelashes are adaptations. Wide feet help the camel to walk in deep sand. Long eyelashes help to keep sand out of the camel's eyes.

What is camouflage?

Camouflage is an **adaptation** that helps animals to hide. The colour of an animal's skin, fur, or feathers may match the things around it.

The colour of this thick-billed lark is the same as the rocky ground where it lives.

A stick insect is difficult to see on a branch! Can you see this one?

The shape of an animal may camouflage it, too. A stick insect is the same shape and colour as a stick. Why do you think animals need to hide?

Animals that eat other animals are called **predators**. **Camouflage** helps them catch food. Animals that predators eat are called **prey**. Camouflage helps prey animals to hide from predators!

Lynx eat other animals. Their spotted fur helps to camouflage them as they hunt.

Find the desert animals

Meerkat

Meerkats sleep in underground homes called **burrows**. In the morning, they go outside to find food. The meerkats' brown fur makes it hard for predators to see them.

CAMOUFLAGED

Meerkats live in groups. They take turns to watch for danger. If a meerkat spots a **predator**, it makes a special call. This call warns the other meerkats.

REVEALED

CAMOUFLAGED

Desert tortoise

Desert tortoises' shells are grey, brown, or black. The **patterns** on the desert tortoises' shells **blend in** with the ground. This helps the tortoises to hide.

Desert tortoises live in rocky or sandy places. Like meerkats, desert tortoises live underground. This keeps them out of the desert heat.

REVEALED

Scorpion

Scorpions have hard bodies with claws. They have four pairs of legs. Scorpions' bodies **blend in** with sand and rocks.

CAMOUFLAGED

Many animals eat scorpions. Can you see how a scorpion's **camouflage** may help it to escape from **predators** – and **survive**?

REVEALED

Roadrunner

Roadrunners are birds that spend most of the time on the ground. Animals such as hawks and cats hunt them. A roadrunner's feathers help it to **blend in** with soil and dry grasses.

Roadrunners can run very quickly. This helps them catch their **prey**. Roadrunners eat lizards, scorpions, and small birds. Sometimes they even eat rattlesnakes!

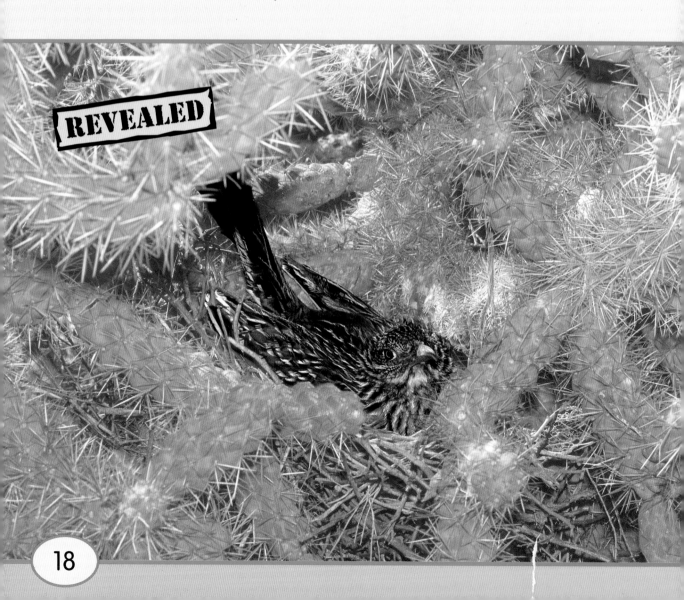

REVEALED

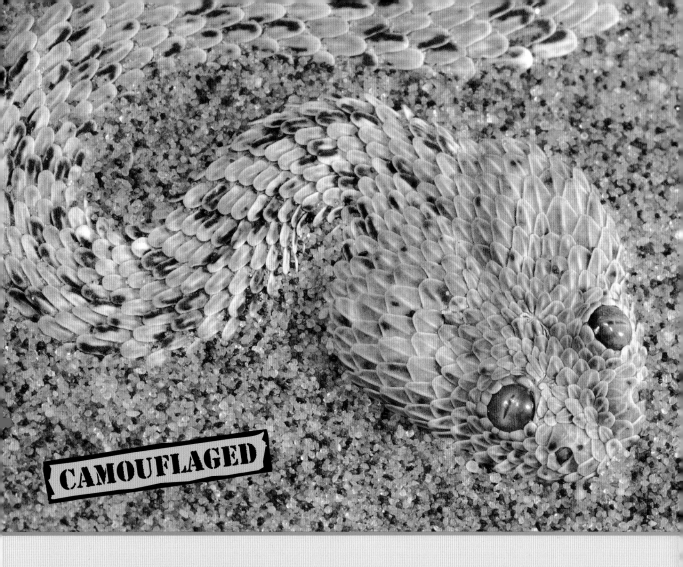

CAMOUFLAGED

Dwarf puff adder

Dwarf puff adders live in deserts in Africa. The **pattern** on their skin helps them to hide. They bury themselves in the sand and wait for prey.

Dwarf puff adders have eyes on top of their heads. This means they can see while they hide. When a lizard comes near, the snake slithers out for a meal.

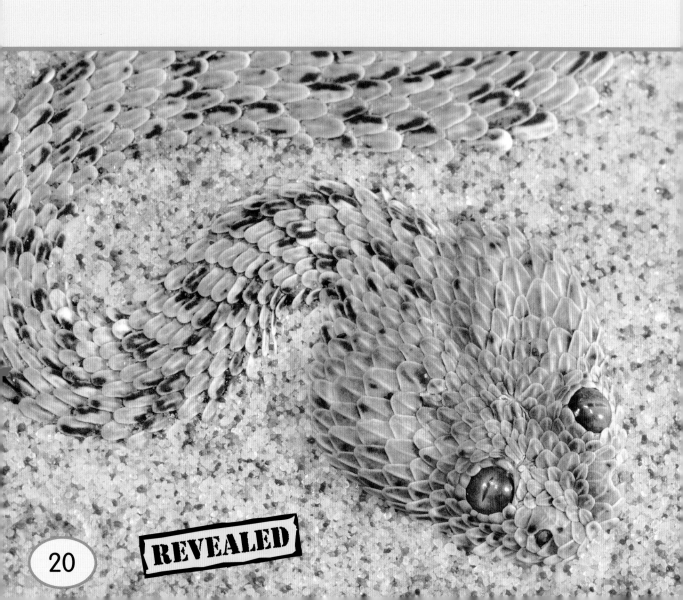

REVEALED

CAMOUFLAGED

Elf owl

Elf owls are the smallest owls in the world. They are only about 13 centimetres tall. Their grey-brown feathers help to **camouflage** them.

If an animal comes near, an elf owl may turn sideways. This hides its lighter parts. The owl may also raise its wing to hide its face.

REVEALED

African bullfrog

African bullfrogs have dull green skin. It helps them to **blend in** while they wait for **prey**. It also helps them hide from birds that might eat them.

The African bullfrog is one of the largest frogs in the world. The frogs eat many different kinds of animals. Sometimes they even eat other bullfrogs! This one is cooling off and hiding in the sand.

REVEALED

Thorny devil

The thorny devil lizard is covered with sharp spikes. It looks like a desert plant. The spikes and **patterns** on its skin help it to hide from hungry birds.

The thorny devil may look scary. However, it is not dangerous – unless you are an ant! Thorny devils can eat hundreds of ants in a single meal.

REVEALED

A squirrel sits on a desert cactus.

Many desert animals have **camouflage**. Their camouflage helps them to **survive**. If you visit a desert, look hard. If you are lucky, you may see some of them!

Animals that stand out

Not all desert animals use **camouflage**. It would be hard to miss the gila monster's bright colours! This lizard has a **venomous** bite. Its colours warn other animals to stay away.

The African coral snake has bright bands of black and yellow. Why doesn't it need to hide? Like the gila monster, it has a venomous bite.

Glossary

adaptation special feature that helps an animal survive in its surroundings

blend in matches well with the things around it

burrow animal's underground home

camouflage adaptation that helps an animal blend in with the things around it

feature special part of an animal

pattern shapes and marks on an animal's skin, fur, shell, or feathers

predator animal that eats other animals

prey animal that other animals eat

stem upright part of a plant

survive stay alive

venomous something dangerous that can make you very ill, or even kill you

Find out more

Books to read

Animals: A Children's Encyclopedia
  (Dorling Kindersley, 2008)

Desert Animals (Who Lives Here?), Deborah Hodge
  and Pat Stevens (Kids Can Press, 2008)

Focus on Habitats: Desert Animals, Stephen Savage
  (Wayland, 2006)

Websites

**gowild.wwf.org.uk/gowild/happening_
habitats/deserts**
Learn more about deserts on the World Wildlife
Fund's Go Wild website.

www.desertanimals.net
Find out more about some of the desert animals in
this book.

Index